Instant .NET 4.5 Extension Methods How-to

Utilize and harness the power of extension methods in your .NET applications

Shawn R. McLean

PUBLISHING

BIRMINGHAM - MUMBAI

Instant .NET 4.5 Extension Methods How-to

First published: April 2013

Production Reference: 1170413

Published by Packt Publishing Ltd.
Livery Place
35 Livery Street
Birmingham B3 2PB, UK.

ISBN 978-1-84968-856-7

www.packtpub.com

Credits

Author
Shawn R. McLean

Reviewer
Wei Chung, Low

IT Content Commissioning Editor
James Jones

Commissioning Editor
Sharvari Tawde

Technical Editor
Worrell Lewis

Project Coordinator
Sherin Padayatty

Proofreader
Linda Morris

Production Coordinator
Shantanu Zagade

Cover Work
Shantanu Zagade

Cover Image
Sheetal Aute

About the Author

Shawn R. McLean is passionate about architecting and developing scalable mobile and web applications based on the Microsoft .NET platform using ASP.NET MVC, ASP.NET WebAPI, and C#, along with using open source frameworks. He is an advocate of software and builds engineering methodologies for a streamlined development process. Besides his love for software engineering, architecture, and design, he also focuses on artificial intelligence and has interest in researching on computer vision and machine learning.

In 2008, he was a gold medalist in the web design category of World Skills Jamaica and a Best of Nation awardee for World Skills International, 2009. In 2009, he was also a finalist for the Microsoft Imagine Cup software design competition in Egypt, where he was the team lead of four, successfully clearing three rounds in a competition of more than 15 teams from around the Central Caribbean. In 2010, he led his team to first place of the Imagine Cup Interoperability award in Poland. He is also the recipient of Jamaica's Prime Minister's Youth Awards, Governor General's iBelieve award, the Gleaner award, and the Chamber of Commerce award for outstanding innovation in the field of technology and science.

He is currently employed by the University Information System Services division of Northern Caribbean University, where he is part of a software engineering team that builds student and learning management systems for universities and high schools. He is also the co-founder of Xormis, a start-up software engineering company that makes in-house mobile and web-based applications for commercial use.

I would like to thank my family and friends for giving me the space and time to work on this book.

About the Reviewer

Wei Chung, Low is a Business Intelligence Manager, a .NET developer, and a MCT, MCPD, MCITP, MCTS, MCSD.NET. He works with IPG MediaBrands (NYSE: IPG) at its Kuala Lumpur, Malaysia campus. He is also a member of PMI, certified as PMP. He started working on Microsoft .NET early in his career and has been involved in development, consultation, and corporate training in the areas of business intelligence, system integration, and virtualization. He has worked for the Bursa Malaysia (formerly Kuala Lumpur Stock Exchange) and Shell IT International previously, which gave him rich integration experiences across different platforms.

He strongly believes that a good system implementation delivers precious value to businesses, and integration of various systems across different platforms shall always be a part of it, just as diverse people from different cultures live together in harmony in most of the major cities.

www.PacktPub.com

Support files, eBooks, discount offers and more

You might want to visit www.PacktPub.com for support files and downloads related to your book.

Did you know that Packt offers eBook versions of every book published, with PDF and ePub files available? You can upgrade to the eBook version at www.PacktPub.com and as a print book customer, you are entitled to a discount on the eBook copy. Get in touch with us at service@packtpub.com for more details.

At www.PacktPub.com, you can also read a collection of free technical articles, sign up for a range of free newsletters and receive exclusive discounts and offers on Packt books and eBooks.

http://PacktLib.PacktPub.com

Do you need instant solutions to your IT questions? PacktLib is Packt's online digital book library. Here, you can access, read and search across Packt's entire library of books.

Why Subscribe?

- Fully searchable across every book published by Packt
- Copy and paste, print and bookmark content
- On demand and accessible via web browser

Free Access for Packt account holders

If you have an account with Packt at www.PacktPub.com, you can use this to access PacktLib today and view nine entirely free books. Simply use your login credentials for immediate access.

Table of Contents

Preface

Instant .NET 4.5 Extension Methods How-to seeks to discover the creation and usage of extension methods from the most basic to veteran coder level of experience. It seeks to improve code maintainability and the structure of your .NET applications. It will take you through a number of clear, practical recipes that will help you take advantage of the power extension methods has to provide in a quick and seamless manner.

What this book covers

Your first extension method (Must know) starts off by creating the simplest form of extension methods and comparing it to the previous way of accomplishing this goal. We go into the technicalities of how the compiler handles extension methods and what they really are.

Extension methods on string data types (Must know) teaches how to extend the string data type for validation and modifications. The various caveats when working with strings are also explained.

Extension methods on classes (Should know) talks about extending your own classes or classes whose source you have no access to.

Chaining extension methods (Should know) talks about writing extension methods in a manner that allows chaining calls when using it.

Overloading extension methods (Should know) shows how to overload your own and existing extension methods.

Overriding extension methods (Should know) aims at teaching the tricks needed to override extension methods and explains its technicalities.

Extension methods on interfaces (Should know) gives examples of creating and using extension methods on interfaces with a twist to mixing it with overloading class extension methods.

Extension methods on enumerables (Should know) aims at showing many tricks of extending enumerables with modifying, filtering, and chaining.

Extension methods on IQueryable (Become an expert) aims at showing performance optimizations and tricks between IEnumerable and IQueryable.

Extension methods with generics (Become an expert) seeks to explore the caveats of extending generics. Extending generics should be done with care, and if not done properly will cause ambiguity when using them.

Extension methods with lambda expressions (Become an expert) talks about extending lambda expressions, that are somewhat of a niche feature and rarely done, and can be very useful for those familiar with the functional programming paradigm.

Structuring your project and best practices (Should know) helps the developer structure their project so it can be easily maintained.

Appendix – List of well-known extension libraries contains a list of useful extension method libraries that developers can include in their projects and get start using them immediately.

What you need for this book

To run the code in this book you need the following:

1. Visual Studio 2008 or higher
2. .NET 3.5 or higher

Who this book is for

This book is great for both new and veteran developers in C# and the .NET framework. The readers are assumed to have basic understanding of the language syntax, types, and OOP concepts. Readers are also expected to have some experience in finding their way around Visual Studio.

Conventions

In this book, you will find a number of styles of text that distinguish between different kinds of information. Here are some examples of these styles, and an explanation of their meaning.

Code words in text are shown as follows: "The only difference between the two code snippets is the keyword `this` in the first parameter."

A block of code is set as follows:

```
//----We use the method like this
int num = 5;
bool isNumEven = false;
//calling the extension method
isNumEven = num.IsEven();
//calling the extension method on raw values
bool isSixEven = 6.IsEven();
```

New terms and **important words** are shown in bold. Words that you see on the screen, in menus or dialog boxes for example, appear in the text like this: "clicking the **Next** button moves you to the next screen".

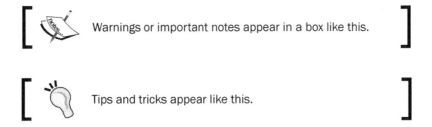

Warnings or important notes appear in a box like this.

Tips and tricks appear like this.

Reader feedback

Feedback from our readers is always welcome. Let us know what you think about this book—what you liked or may have disliked. Reader feedback is important for us to develop titles that you really get the most out of.

To send us general feedback, simply send an e mail to feedback@packtpub.com, and mention the book title via the subject of your message.

If there is a topic that you have expertise in and you are interested in either writing or contributing to a book, see our author guide on www.packtpub.com/authors.

Customer support

Now that you are the proud owner of a Packt book, we have a number of things to help you to get the most from your purchase.

Downloading the example code

You can download the example code files for all Packt books you have purchased from your account at http://www.packtpub.com. If you purchased this book elsewhere, you can visit http://www.packtpub.com/support and register to have the files e-mailed directly to you.

Errata

Although we have taken every care to ensure the accuracy of our content, mistakes do happen. If you find a mistake in one of our books—maybe a mistake in the text or the code—we would be grateful if you would report this to us. By doing so, you can save other readers from frustration and help us improve subsequent versions of this book. If you find any errata, please report them by visiting http://www.packtpub.com/submit-errata, selecting your book, clicking on the **errata submission form** link, and entering the details of your errata. Once your errata are verified, your submission will be accepted and the errata will be uploaded on our website, or added to any list of existing errata, under the Errata section of that title. Any existing errata can be viewed by selecting your title from http://www.packtpub.com/support.

Piracy

Piracy of copyright material on the Internet is an ongoing problem across all media. At Packt, we take the protection of our copyright and licenses very seriously. If you come across any illegal copies of our works, in any form, on the Internet, please provide us with the location address or website name immediately so that we can pursue a remedy.

Please contact us at copyright@packtpub.com with a link to the suspected pirated material.

We appreciate your help in protecting our authors, and our ability to bring you valuable content.

Questions

You can contact us at questions@packtpub.com if you are having a problem with any aspect of the book, and we will do our best to address it.

Instant .NET 4.5 Extension Methods How-to

Welcome to *.NET Extension Methods How-to*. Here, we will cover how to create and use extension methods ranging from simple string extensions to complex LINQ extensions. It should be noted that this feature of the C# language was implemented in Version 3.0.

Your first extension method (Must know)

Extension methods allow the developer to add their own method to an existing type, without creating a derived type or modifying the existing type. They are mostly suited for cases in which the developer wishes to add additional functionality to existing classes where they may have no access to the source code, such as .NET framework classes found in namespaces like `System` and Microsoft. In this recipe, we will create our first simple extension method.

The second step, after learning to write "Hello world", is to do arithmetic and logic, for example you might need to check if a number is odd or even. The usual way would be to define a utility class and add a method to it. We'll also write an extension method to do this, which will make your code cleaner and well structured. In this recipe, we will look at two ways to write helper methods; using the static method utility way and the extension method way for checking if a number is even or not.

The following screenshot shows the structure of our projects when extension methods are written:

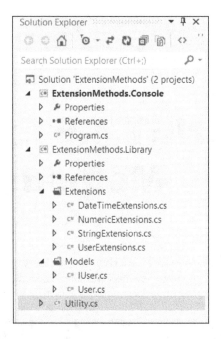

Getting ready

All code in this book is also available in the supporting code files online for a more complete and integrated understanding. The code files is a Visual Studio solution with two projects; ExtensionMethods.Console that contains the implementations of the extensions and ExtensionMethods.Library that contains the extensions.

For this recipe, refer to the NumericExtensions.cs and Utility.cs files in the ExtensionMethods.Library project for the extension method. These methods are used in the Program.cs file in the ExtensionMethods.Console project.

How to do it...

The following code shows the Utility class way of checking if a number is even:

```
public class Utility
{
    /// <summary>
    /// Utility method that checks if a number is even
    /// </summary>
    /// <param name="val"></param>
```

```
    /// <returns></returns>
    public static bool IsEven(int val)
    {
        return val%2 == 0;
    }
}


//----We use the method like this:
int num = 5;
bool isNumEven = false;
//utility class method
isNumEven = Utility.IsEven(num);
```

The following code shows the extension method way of checking if a number is even:

```
public static class NumericExtensions
{
    /// <summary>
    /// Extension method that checks if the number is even
    /// </summary>
    /// <param name="val"></param>
    /// <returns></returns>
    public static bool IsEven(this int val)
    {
        return val % 2 == 0;
    }
}
```

The following code shows how we use the static method and extension method:

```
//----We use the method like this
int num = 5;
bool isNumEven = false;
//calling the extension method
isNumEven = num.IsEven();
//calling the extension method on raw values
bool isSixEven = 6.IsEven();
```

How it works...

In the first code snippet, we have an `IsEven` static method that accepts the parameter we want to work on. When using this method, we call it through its `Utility` class:

```
isNumEven = Utility.IsEven(num);
```

In the second code snippet, we converted this method into an extension method. We will look into the basics of an extension method, given as follows:

▶ **Syntactic sugar**: An extension method is not part of the type/class; they are really syntactic sugar for static methods. There are no differences in the **Intermediate Language** (**IL**) generated when these two code snippets are compiled.

▶ **"this" differentiation**: The only difference between the two code snippets is the keyword `this` in the first parameter. It tells the compiler that `IsEven` is an extension method for the type (`int`) of that parameter. This allows you to call `IsEven` on any object of type `int`, even if it's in a raw form:

```
bool isSixEven = 6.IsEven();
```

▶ **Implementation**: There is no limit on how an extension method can be implemented. They can perform any operation as any other method, including modifying its instance object (`val`) and returning any type or none at all (`void`).

In this example, we have created and used an extension method in its most primitive form.

Extension methods on string data types (Must know)

Now, it is time to move on to extending the string data type. There are many reasons for extending a string, from validating to manipulation. We will write two extension methods, one manipulating a string by replacing diacritic characters with non-diacritic ones and then validating it. We will also pass a parameter to the second extension to specify what kind of validation it is.

The following image shows us that Visual Studio's IntelliSense will recognize the extension method on the `url` string:

```
//should be false due to Diacritic characters.
bool isValidUrl = url.re
                     ❖ Remove
                     ❖ RemoveDiacritics    (this string value):string
                     ❖ Replace
```

Getting ready

Refer to the `StringExtensions.cs` file in the `ExtensionMethods.Library` project for the extension methods. These methods are used in the `Program.cs` file in the `ExtensionMethods.Console` project.

How to do it...

The following code shows two extension methods, `Validate` and `RemoveDiacritics`:

```
public static bool Validate(this string value, ValidationType type)
{
    switch(type)
    {
        case ValidationType.Email:
            return Regex.IsMatch(value,
                            @"^([0-9a-zA-Z]([\+\-_\.][0-9a-zA-Z]+)*)+@
(([0-9a-zA-Z][-\w]*[0-9a-zA-Z]*\.)+[a-zA-Z0-9]{2,17})$");
        case ValidationType.Url:
            return Uri.IsWellFormedUriString(value, UriKind.
RelativeOrAbsolute);
        default:
            throw new ArgumentOutOfRangeException("type");
    }
}

public static string RemoveDiacritics(this string value)
{
    string stFormD = value.Normalize(NormalizationForm.FormD);
    StringBuilder sb = new StringBuilder();

    for (int ich = 0; ich < stFormD.Length; ich++)
    {
        UnicodeCategory uc = CharUnicodeInfo.GetUnicodeCategory(stFor
mD[ich]);
        if (uc != UnicodeCategory.NonSpacingMark)
        {
            sb.Append(stFormD[ich]);
        }
    }
    return sb.ToString().Normalize(NormalizationForm.FormC);
}
```

The following code shows the use of the extension methods:

```
var url = "http://www.mywebsite.com/articles/éxtenšíoň-methóds";
//should be false due to Diacritic characters.
bool isValidUrl = url.Validate(ValidationType.Url);

//lets remove them now
url = url.RemoveDiacritics();
//should now be: http://www.mywebsite.com/articles/extension-methods

//should now be true
bool isValidUrl1 = url.Validate(ValidationType.Url);
```

How it works...

We have seen how to implement validation on strings and how to pass additional parameters to extension methods as seen in the `Validate` method. The way we did this is to create a method with an enum parameter to tell us the type of validation it is. The implementation of this method uses a simple `switch` statement to determine what validation algorithm to use, it then returns a `bool` value depending on how the validation went.

In the `RemoveDiacritics` method, we attempted to clean a string of diacritic characters, which would not pass as a valid URL. Other string cleaning methods such as HTML encoding and cleaning a string for SQL injection would be well suited as an extension method.

There's more...

Some additional things to note about extension methods on strings are shown as follows:

> ▶ **Passing parameters**: An extension method is just like a normal method and supports parameters in the same way. The second parameter in the definition is the first accepted argument when the method is called:
>
> ```
> //the method definition
> public static bool Validate(this string value, ValidationType
> type)
> //calling the method
> bool isValidUrl = url.Validate(ValidationType.Url);
> ```
>
> ▶ **Manipulation**: Strings are immutable, we will not be able to manipulate the actual string instance that the extension was called on. This is why we returned the manipulated version. In the usages snippet, we assigned the return value back to itself:
>
> ```
> url = url.RemoveDiacritics();
> ```

In this recipe, we have created and used extension methods on the type string.

Extension methods on classes (Should know)

Classes are the core of the C# language and the .NET framework is filled with thousands of classes that we cannot edit, such as the `System.Linq.Enumerable` class. This is where extension methods shine; being able to extend a class without recompiling it or using inheritance. In this recipe, we will extend a custom `User` class to manipulate properties and return a formatted string.

Getting ready

Refer to the `UserExtensions.cs` and `Models/Users.cs` file in the `ExtensionMethods.Library` project for the extension methods and class. These methods are used in the `Program.cs` file in the `ExtensionMethods.Console` project.

How to do it...

The following code shows the custom class we will be working with:

```
public class User
{
    private int _id;

    public int UserId
    {
        get { return _id; }
        set { _id = value; }
    }

    public string FirstName { get; set; }
    public string LastName { get; set; }
}
```

The following code shows two extension methods:

```
/// <summary>
/// Gets the full name of the user by merging all other names if no
FullName is set.
/// </summary>
/// <param name="value"></param>
/// <returns></returns>
public static string GetFullName(this User value)
{
    return string.Format("{0} {1}", value.FirstName, value.LastName);
}
```

```
/// <summary>
/// Parses and set a 2 word name into first and last names
/// </summary>
/// <param name="value"></param>
/// <param name="fullName"></param>
public static void SetNames(this User value, string fullName)
{
    //the default delimiter is whitespace if no params are passed.
    string[] names = fullName.Split();
    value.FirstName = names[0];
    value.LastName = names[1];
}
```

The following code shows shows the use of the extension methods:

```
User user = new User
{
    FirstName = "Shawn",
    LastName = "Mclean"
};
//should be "Shawn Mclean"
string fullName = user.GetFullName();

//user.FirstName should be "Trevoir" and user.LastName "Williams"
user.SetNames("Trevoir Williams");
```

How it works...

Here, we created a `User` class in which we will add additional functionality by using extension methods. The first extension method is `GetFullName` which accesses the object's properties and combines them to return an output. The second extension method is `SetNames`, which actually modifies the properties of the object.

Accessing and modifying object properties and calling public methods of the object inside the extension method is straightforward.

There's more...

There are some key points to note when extending classes:

> ▶ **Privates are inaccessible**: As stated earlier, extension methods are not part of the class; hence, they have no access to the private fields or methods of the object. The following extension method would never work when trying to access a private _id variable:
>
> ```
> public static string GetId(this User value)
> {
> ```

```
//Syntax error would be thrown here.
  return value._id;
}
```

▶ **Modifying the instance object**: When modifying the instance object, ensure not to assign a new instance to the variable, this will lead to a new instance being created for the duration of the extension method's scope and will not actually modify the caller instance. The following is a demonstration of this:

```
public static void ChangeName(this User value, string firstName)
{
  value = new User {
FirstName = firstName,
LastName = value.LastName
};
}
```

The value of `FirstName` in the original instance will still be the same after execution.

In this recipe, we have understood the fundamentals of working with a class and a few quirks.

Chaining extension methods (Should know)

Method chaining, the core concept behind building fluent interfaces is to allow for better readability. The key to method chaining is to have the extension return an instance of the caller. In later recipes, most extension methods you use will be chained extension methods. If you have used jQuery before, then you have experienced method chaining. This recipe should give you the basic understanding of how and when to chain a method.

Getting ready

Refer to the `UserExtensions.cs` and `Models/Users.cs` files in the `ExtensionMethods.Library` project for the extension methods and class. These methods are used in the `Program.cs` file in the `ExtensionMethods.Console` project.

How to do it...

The following code is an upgrade of the previous `SetName` method that allows chaining:

```
/// <summary>
/// This is a chained version of SetNames
/// </summary>
/// <param name="value"></param>
/// <param name="fullName"></param>
```

```
public static User SetNamesChained(this User value, string fullName)
{
    //the default delimiter is whitespace if no params are passed.
    string[] names = fullName.Split();
    value.FirstName = names[0];
    value.LastName = names[1];
    return value;
}
```

The following code shows the use of the extension methods:

```
User user = new User();
string fullName = user.SetNamesChained("Derron Brown").GetFullName();
```

How it works...

Method chaining increases code readability, but makes debugging tricky to accomplish; you cannot put break points at each method call to know the value returned by a particular method or which method threw an exception without examining the stack trace. *We can only chain methods that return its instance.* As seen in the extension usage snippet, we can call another method directly after the `SetNamesChained` method was called.

Method chaining is mainly used in fluent APIs, such as querying or in very verbose situations like validating and testing conditions. An example of testing conditions would be in the `CuttinEdge.Conditions` library:

```
public void GetData(int? id)
{
    Condition.Requires(id, "id")
        .IsNotNull()        // throws ArgumentNullException on failure
        .IsInRange(1, 999) // ArgumentOutOfRangeException on failure
  .IsNotEqualTo(128);// throws ArgumentException on failure
}
```

Now, the code is much more readable. In this recipe, we have learned one of the core features used by LINQ and other query mechanisms which we will use in later recipes.

Overloading extension methods (Should know)

Most OOP languages allow us to have methods with the same name but different parameters, which is known as function overloading. Overloading extension methods is the same as function overloading and follows the same criteria. In this recipe, you will learn function overloading as it relates to extension methods.

The following screenshot shows that Visual Studio's IntelliSense will list all the overloaded extensions on the `user` object:

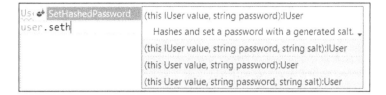

Getting ready

Refer to the `UserExtensions.cs` file in the `ExtensionMethods.Library` project for the extension methods. These methods are used in the `Program.cs` file in the `ExtensionMethods.Console` project.

How to do it...

The following code shows two extension methods; `CreateSalt` and `SetHashedPassword`:

```
/// <summary>
/// Creates a random string of a specific size.
/// </summary>
/// <param name="size"></param>
/// <returns></returns>
private static string CreateSalt(int size)
{
    var rnq = new RNGCryptoServiceProvider();
    var buff = new byte[size];
    rng.GetBytes(buff);
    return Convert.ToBase64String(buff);
}


/// <summary>
/// Hash a string using SHA256Managed Algorithm
/// </summary>
/// <param name="value"></param>
/// <returns></returns>
public static string Hash(string value)
{
    HashAlgorithm algorithm = new SHA256Managed();
    Byte[] inputBytes = Encoding.UTF8.GetBytes(value);

    Byte[] hashedBytes = algorithm.ComputeHash(inputBytes);
```

```
        return BitConverter.ToString(hashedBytes);
}


/// <summary>
/// Hashes and set a password with a generated salt.
/// </summary>
/// <param name="value"></param>
/// <param name="password"></param>
/// <returns></returns>
public static User SetHashedPassword(this User value, string password)
{
    string generatedSalt = CreateSalt(25);

    return SetHashedPassword(value, password, generatedSalt);
}

/// <summary>
/// Hashes and set a password with the salt argument.
/// </summary>
/// <param name="value"></param>
/// <param name="password"></param>
/// <param name="salt"></param>
/// <returns></returns>
public static User SetHashedPassword(this User value, string password,
string salt)
{
    value.Password = Hash(string.Concat(password, salt));
    value.PasswordSalt = salt;
    return value;
}
```

The following code shows the use of the extension methods:

```
User user = new User();
user.SetHashedPassword("samplepassword");

User user1 = new User();
user1.SetHashedPassword("samplepassword", "myownsalt");
```

How it works...

In the code snippets, we have added two extension methods (SetHashedPassword) for hashing and setting a password.

The first method only takes a password parameter, generates a salt by calling another static method, then passes the password and salt to the second extension method that will handle the hashing and modification of the properties. You may have noticed that we called the second extension method as a normal static method:

```
return SetHashedPassword(value, password, generatedSalt);
```

Here are some additional information to consider when overloading extension methods:

> **Criteria for overloading**: The compiler will verify that a method is overloaded based on the argument type or the number of arguments and that they have the same name. The return type is *not* considered in the function signature.

> **Calling an overloaded extension**: The decision of which method is called is made at compile time, based on the parameters that you used when calling it. Visual Studio's IntelliSense will also give you an idea of what overloads are available to you.

Try to limit the number of overloaded methods, as this causes confusion to the developer using these methods.

In this recipe, you have learned how to create and use overloaded extension methods.

Overriding extension methods (Should know)

Extension methods *cannot* be overridden the way classes and instance methods are. They are overridden by a slight trick in how the compiler selects which extension method to use by using "closeness" of the method to the caller via namespaces. In this recipe, you will learn how to manipulate the namespace to get the correct extension method you wish to use.

Getting ready

Refer to the `StringExtensions.cs` file in the `ExtensionMethods.Library` project for the extension methods. These methods are used in the `Program.cs` file in the `ExtensionMethods.Console` project.

How to do it...

The following code shows two extension methods, `Shuffle`, in two separate namespaces:

```
namespace ExtensionMethods.Library
{
    public static class StringExtensions
    {
        public static string Shuffle(this string value)
        {
            char[] array = value.ToCharArray();
            Random rnd = new Random();
```

```
                        return string.Concat(array.OrderBy(x => rnd.Next()));
                }
        }
}


namespace UnknownExtensions
{
    public static class StringExtensions
    {
        public static string Shuffle(this string value)
        {
            char[] array = value.ToCharArray();
            Random rng = new Random();
            int n = array.Length;
            while (n > 1)
            {
                n--;
                int k = rng.Next(n + 1);
                var val = array[k];
                array[k] = array[n];
                array[n] = val;
            }
            return new string(array);
        }
    }
}
```

The following code shows the use of the extension methods:

```
namespace ExtensionMethods.Console
{
    using ExtensionMethods.Library;
    internal class Program
    {
        private static void Main(string[] args)
        {
            DoTaskSix();
            MyNamespace.Program.DoTaskSixUpgraded();
        }

        private static void DoTaskSix()
        {
            System.Console.WriteLine("inefficient shuffle".Shuffle());
        }
    }
```

```
namespace MyNamespace
{
    using UnknownExtensions;
    internal static class Program
    {
        public static void DoTaskSixUpgraded()
        {
            System.Console.WriteLine("efficient shuffle".
Shuffle());
        }
    }
}
}
```

How it works...

In the code snippet, we have two extension methods, one in our typical `ExtensionMethods.Library` namespace and one in a new `UnknownExtensions` namespace. Both extensions are given the same name, but are implemented differently.

In the code snippet where we used these methods, we called the extension method normally in `DoTaskSix` where the `using ExtensionMethods.Library;` line is directly applied to the caller. To call the new extension method added outside of our normal namespace, we had to declare a new namespace (`MyNamespace`) and include `using UnknownExtensions` for that scope.

▶ **Name spacing**: You can change which extension method is called by ensuring that the namespace it is in is closer, or in the same namespace of the caller. We can also make the compiler select the extension directly by the `using` keyword as seen in the preceding code snippet. However, if we have an extension method in both namespaces that are being used in the same scope, we will end up with an ambiguous method error from the compiler:

```
using ExtensionMethods.Library;
using UnknownExtensions;
```

Avoid creating extension methods in the same namespace as other instance methods or extension methods, as future updates might implement a method with the same signature and break your code.

▶ **Instance methods**: Instance methods *cannot* be overridden. An extension method with the same signature as an instance method will, however, compile without errors but will not take precedence over the instance method during compilation. The `GetHashCode` method is one such example that cannot be overridden. Remember, extension methods are just the compiler facilitating static methods.

In this recipe, you have learned how to implement and use overridden extension methods. No form of this is recommended, unless it is completely required after redesigning or refactoring your code.

Extension methods on interfaces (Should know)

Extension methods can also be used to extend interfaces. This may seem unorthodox when thinking with a strict OOP mindset, as extension methods include implementation while interfaces will contain the method prototypes. In this recipe, we have extracted an interface from the `User` class in the previous recipes and written extension methods for the interface itself.

Getting ready

Refer to the `UserExtensions.cs` and `Models/IUser.cs` files in the `ExtensionMethods.Library` project for the extension methods and interfaces. These methods are used in the `Program.cs` file in the `ExtensionMethods.Console` project.

How to do it...

The following code shows the two rewritten extension methods:

```
/// <summary>
/// Hashes and set a password with a generated salt.
/// </summary>
/// <param name="value"></param>
/// <param name="password"></param>
/// <returns></returns>
public static IUser SetHashedPassword(this IUser value, string
password)
{
    string generatedSalt = CreateSalt(25);

    return SetHashedPassword(value, password, generatedSalt);
}

/// <summary>
/// Hashes and set a password with the salt argument.
/// </summary>
/// <param name="value"></param>
/// <param name="password"></param>
/// <param name="salt"></param>
/// <returns></returns>
```

```csharp
public static IUser SetHashedPassword(this IUser value, string
password, string salt)
{
    value.Password = Hash(string.Concat(password, salt));
    value.PasswordSalt = salt;
    return value;
}
```

The interface extracted from the class:

```csharp
public class Student : IUser
{
    public int UserId { get; set; }
    public string FirstName { get; set; }
    public string LastName { get; set; }
    public string Password { get; set; }
    public string PasswordSalt { get; set; }
    public DateTime DateOfBirth { get; set; }
}


public class Teacher : IUser
{
    public int UserId { get; set; }
    public string FirstName { get; set; }
    public string LastName { get; set; }
    public string Password { get; set; }
    public string PasswordSalt { get; set; }
    public string TaughtSubject { get; set; }
}
```

The following code shows the use of the extension methods:

```csharp
Teacher user = new Teacher();
user.SetHashedPassword("samplepassword");

Student user1 = new Student();
user1.SetHashedPassword("samplepassword", "myownsalt");
```

How it works...

Our first step was to extract the IUser interface from our previous User class. We then created two classes, Student and Teacher, which inherits from the IUser interface. Extension methods (SetHashedPassword) were created based on IUser. Calling the extension can be done on any object that implements the IUser interface.

The compiler will use the closest method to the object type, a concept similar to what we did in the *Overriding extension methods* recipe. If we create an extension method for the `Student` class, then the compiler will select that extension method to be called instead of the method for the interface.

Extension methods on interfaces are straightforward if you understand how to create them for classes.

Extension methods on enumerables (Should know)

Now, we move on to where extension methods are used the most, enumerated types. In an article by *Eric Lippert*, a principal developer on the C# team; LINQ was the reason extension methods were created in the first place. In this recipe, we will look at writing our own extension methods for the `IEnumerable` and `IList` type and take a look at an existing extension method in the .NET framework from the LINQ namespace.

Getting ready

Refer to the `IEnumerableExtensions.cs` and `IListExtensions.cs` file in the `ExtensionMethods.Library` project for the extension methods. These methods are used in the `IEnumerableExtensionTests.cs` file in the `ExtensionMethods.Tests` project.

How to do it...

The following code snippet shows the extension method `Count()` from the LINQ namespace:

```
public static int Count<TSource>(this IEnumerable<TSource> source)
{
    if (source == null)
    {
        throw Error.ArgumentNull("source");
    }
    ICollection<TSource> is2 = source as ICollection<TSource>;
    if (is2 != null)
    {
        return is2.Count;
    }
    int num = 0;
    using (IEnumerator<TSource> enumerator = source.GetEnumerator())
```

```
    {
        while (enumerator.MoveNext())
        {
            num++;
        }
    }
    return num;
}
```

The following code is our custom code snippet of an extension method for using bubble sort on an IList:

```
/// <summary>
/// Sort list using bubble sort algorithm
/// </summary>
/// <typeparam name="T"></typeparam>
/// <param name="list"></param>
public static void BubbleSort<T>(this IList<T> list) where T :
IComparable
{
    BubbleSort(list, 0, list.Count - 1);
}
/// <summary>
/// Sort list using bubble sort algorithm
/// </summary>
/// <typeparam name="T"></typeparam>
/// <param name="list"></param>
/// <param name="startIndex">starting index</param>
/// <param name="endIndex">end index</param>
public static void BubbleSort<T>(this IList<T> list,
        int startIndex, int endIndex) where T : IComparable
{
    //Bubble Sort
    for (int i = startIndex; i < endIndex; i++)
        for (int j = endIndex; j > i; j--)
            if (list[j].IsLesserThan(list[j - 1]))
                list.Exchange(j, j - 1);
}
/// <summary>
/// Swap values of list by index
/// </summary>
/// <typeparam name="T"></typeparam>
/// <param name="list"></param>
/// <param name="index1">1st index to swap with 2nd index</param>
/// <param name="index2">2nd index to swap with 1st index</param>
```

```
private static void Exchange<T>(this IList<T> list, int index1, int
index2)
{
    T tmp = list[index1];
    list[index1] = list[index2];
    list[index2] = tmp;
}
private static bool IsLesserThan(this IComparable value, IComparable
item)
{
    return value.CompareTo(item) < 0;
}
```

The following code snippet is our custom extension method for counting a sorted
IEnumerable:

```
public static class IEnumerableExtensions
{
    public static int CountSorted<T>(this IEnumerable<T> values, T
item) where T : IComparable
    {
        //convert to list to operate on it better.
        var list = values.ToList();

        //find random index of the item
        int index = list.BinarySearch(item);

        //if item isn't found, just return -1
        if (index < 0)
            return -1;


        int leftEdge = findLeftEdge(list, 0, index, item, Comparer<T>.
Default);
        int rightEdge = findRightEdge(list, index, list.Count - 1,
item, Comparer<T>.Default);

        //count it by taking away the left from the right
        return rightEdge - leftEdge + 1;
    }}
```

The following code snippets show how to implement these extension methods:

```
[TestMethod]
public void BubbleSortTest()
{
    IList<int> list = new List<int> { 3, 2, 1 };
    list.BubbleSort();
    Assert.IsTrue(new List<int>{1,2,3}.SequenceEqual(list));
}
[TestMethod]
public void BubbleSort_And_Count_Test()
{
    IList<int> list = new List<int> { 3,2,1,2 };
    int count = list.BubbleSort().CountSorted(2);
    Assert.AreEqual(2,count);
}
```

How it works...

The first code snippet of `Count()` was taken from the .NET framework `System.Linq` namespace using a decompile tool. The `System.Linq` namespace is filled with extension methods for enumerated types such as `IEnumerable`. This is an example that demonstrates that even the owners of classes can create extension methods for the sake of maintainability of the projects.

Our second code snippet is `BubbleSort` for the `IList` interface type. The algorithm operates on the instance object and sorts it using the bubble sort algorithm. This extension method has rules that govern what `T` should be, and should be inherited from the `IComparable` type or any type that can be compared, so that the algorithm can know which items are greater and smaller.

Our third code snippet `CountSorted` is used on sorted enumerable types using a modified binary search for an optimized count. This public method also calls private static functions which follows proper object-oriented guidelines.

There's more...

When working with enumerated types, there are a few key points to keep in mind:

▶ **Inheritance**: In the `BubbleSort_And_Count_Test` method, we chained the `CountSorted` extension method (extending `IEnumerable`) on an `IList` type. This is possible as `IList` inherits from `IEnumerable`, whatever we can do on `IEnumerable`, we can also do on `IList`.

```
int count = list.BubbleSort().CountSorted(2);
```

> ▸ **Manipulation**: The `BubbleSort` extension method worked directly on the list it was operating on. As with classes, the list is passed by reference and can be manipulated. In the `BubbleSortTest` method, there was no need to assign it back to itself after calling the method.
>
> ```
> IList<int> list = new List<int> { 3, 2, 1 };
>     list.BubbleSort(); //list is now sorted as {1,2,3}
> ```
>
> ▸ **Private extensions**: In the `IEnumerableExtensions` class, we utilized both public and private extension methods so our class file can be properly structured. Both work just the same with the difference of public and private access.
>
> ```
> private static void Exchange<T>(this IList<T> list, int index1,
>     int index2)
> ```

You will find that most of the extension methods you write will be operating on enumerated types.

Extension methods on IQueryable (Become an expert)

IQueryable is used to operate mainly on databases. `IQueryable<T>` are an extension from `IEnumerable<T>`, hence, we can call all extensions and methods of `IEnumerable<T>`. A query using IQueryable can be built up on over time, before it hits the database. The query is executed once you execute an eager function such as `ToList()`, looping the data or attempting to use the values. IQueryable is used by providers such as LINQ to entities or LINQ to SQL.

Getting ready

Refer to the `IQueryableExtensions.cs` file in the `ExtensionMethods.Library` project for the extension methods. The models are located in `Models/PagedList.cs` and `Models/IPagedList.cs`. These methods are used in the `IQueryableExtensionTests.cs` file in the `ExtensionMethods.Tests` project.

How to do it...

The following code snippet shows a general use of extension methods on IQueryables:

```
public static User ByUserId(this IQueryable<User> query, int userId)
{
    return query.First(u => u.UserId == userId);
}
```

The following code snippet is a paged list class for pagination of data:

```
public class PagedList<T> : List<T>, IPagedList
{
    public PagedList(IQueryable<T> source, int index, int pageSize)
    {
        this.TotalCount = source.Count();
        this.PageSize = pageSize;
        this.PageIndex = index;
        this.AddRange(source.Skip(index * pageSize).Take(pageSize).
ToList());
    }

    public PagedList(List<T> source, int index, int pageSize)
    {
        this.TotalCount = source.Count();
        this.PageSize = pageSize;
        this.PageIndex = index;
        this.AddRange(source.Skip(index * pageSize).Take(pageSize).
ToList());
    }

    public int TotalCount
    {
        get; set;
    }

    public int PageIndex
    {
        get; set;
    }

    public int PageSize
    {
        get; set;
    }

    public bool IsPreviousPage
    {
        get
        {
            return (PageIndex > 0);
        }
    }
    public bool IsNextPage
```

```
    {
        get
        {
            return (PageIndex * PageSize) <=TotalCount;
        }
    }
}
```

The following code snippet is the extension method that executes and converts the query to the `PagedList` object:

```
public static PagedList<T> ToPagedList<T>(this IQueryable<T> source,
int index, int pageSize)
{
    return new PagedList<T>(source, index, pageSize);
}
```

The following code snippet shows how we use these extension methods:

```
[TestMethod]
public void UserByIdReturnsCorrectUser()
{
    var query = new List<User>
                    {
                        new User {UserId = 1},
                        new User {UserId = 2}
                    }.AsQueryable();

    var user = query.ByUserId(1);

    Assert.AreEqual(1, user.UserId);
}


[TestMethod]
public void PagedList_Contains_Correct_Number_Of_Elements()
{
    var query = new List<int>{1,2,3,4,5,6,7,8,9,10}.AsQueryable();

    var pagedList = query.ToPagedList(0, 5);

    Assert.AreEqual(5, pagedList.Count);
    Assert.AreEqual(10, pagedList.TotalCount);
}
```

How it works...

The first code snippet `ByUserId` is the most commonly used type of extension method for IQueryable types. An alternative to this method is to use the repository pattern and add a method of getting a user by the Id. But sometimes, we will expose the query to lower levels of the app such as the service layer where we might need to use this feature at multiple places, hence refactoring that logic into an extension method makes perfect sense.

This extension method evaluates and executes the query immediately due to requesting a single value using the `First()` method:

```
query.First(u => u.UserId == userId);
```

The second code snippet gives us a `PagedList` model which becomes a valuable class when working with grids or pagination. The constructor accepts an IQueryable or IList and converts that data into a paged list. Take note of the line in which we evaluate the source by calling `ToList()`. This line executes the query on the provider:

```
this.AddRange(source.Skip(index * pageSize).Take(pageSize).ToList());
```

In the code snippets using these extension methods, we have created a list and cast it to an IQueryable type. This is purely for the purpose of demonstration. In a real application, the query would be coming from a LINQ to SQL or entities context, which is in charge of executing the query against a database.

We need to be careful of how extension methods on IQueryable are written. A poorly written query will result in unexpected behavior, such as premature query execution. If the extension method is simply building up the query (using method chaining), ensure that the query is not evaluated inside the method. If the query is evaluated and executed before the method finishes, any other use of the query outside of the extension method will result in operating on the data in memory.

In this recipe, you have learned a few tricks and caveats when using extending IQueryable.

Extension methods with generics (Become an expert)

Generics in C# allows us to create type-safe definitions of methods and classes without the actual need to commit to an actual data type. You have worked with generic types in the previous recipe, such as enumerated data types and, soon, lambda expression. Generic types can be extended, as shown in the previous recipe; however, there are a few caveats you should keep in mind when extending generics that we will cover in this recipe.

Getting ready

Refer to the `GenericExtensions.cs` and `Models/Users.cs` files in the `ExtensionMethods.Library` project for the extension methods and class. These methods are used in the `Program.cs` file in the `ExtensionMethods.Console` project.

How to do it...

The following code shows the `Serialize` and `SerializeUser` extension methods that we are using:

```
public static class GenericExtensions
{
    /// <summary>
    /// Serializes an object to json string
    /// </summary>
    /// <typeparam name="T"></typeparam>
    /// <param name="entity"></param>
    /// <returns></returns>
    public static string Serialize<T>(this T entity)
    {
        return JsonConvert.SerializeObject(entity);
    }
    /// <summary>
    /// Serializes any type inheriting from IUser to json string.
    /// </summary>
    /// <typeparam name="T"></typeparam>
    /// <param name="entity"></param>
    /// <returns></returns>
    public static string SerializeUser<T>(this T entity) where T :
IUser
    {
        //remove password from the object
        entity.Password = string.Empty;
        return JsonConvert.SerializeObject(entity);
    }
}
```

The following code shows the use of these extension methods:

```
[TestClass]
public class GenericExtensionTests
{
    [TestMethod]
    public void SerializeObjectTest()
```

```
    {
        var obj = new User
                        {
                            FirstName = "Cheyenne",
                            LastName = "Powell",
                            Password = "test"
                        };
        string json = obj.Serialize();
        Assert.IsTrue(json.Contains("test"));
    }


    [TestMethod]
    public void Serialize_IUser_Object_Test()
    {
        var obj = new User
        {
            FirstName = "Cheyenne",
            LastName = "Powell",
            Password = "test"
        };
        string json = obj.SerializeUser();
        //SerializeUser should remove the password
        Assert.IsFalse(json.Contains("test"));
    }
}
```

How it works...

In the first snippet, we have the `Serialize` extension method on the generic type T. The purpose of this extension is to serialize an object to a JSON string. This means that this method can be executed on any type.

The following screenshot shows that the IntelliSense treats this as an `object` type:

Be careful of infinite recursions as you may notice that the method is also available to be called again.

When using this extension method, you may find that it can be called on *any* type, including strings, integers, and so on. This may cause unintended behaviors and could be, potentially, dangerous.

The second code snippet gives us an upgraded and safer version of this method. `SerializeUser` utilizes the `where` clause to place a condition on the type of generic data type this method is exposed to:

```
public static string SerializeUser<T>(this T entity) where T : IUser
```

This clause states that this method is only available to those objects that are of type `IUser`, or inherits from it. In the previous screenshot, you will notice that this extension method is not available to that data type in the IntelliSense. Even though our parameter `entity` is of type `T`, the clause tells the compiler it is actually an `IUser` type, the IntelliSense will operate accordingly.

The purpose of our `SerializeUser` method is to serialize the object of the `IUser` type while removing the password from it. In the following image, both methods are available to us in IntelliSense. The compiler sees that `obj` is of the `User` type which inherits from the `IUser` type which tells the IntelliSense to show us `SerializeUser`.

The following screenshot shows the IntelliSense being activated and displays the available methods for both the `object` and `IUser` type:

```
[TestMethod]
public void Serialize_IUser_Object_Test()
{
    var obj = new User
    {
        FirstName = "Cheyenne",
        LastName = "Powell",
        Password = '    Serialize
    };                      SerializeUser    (this T entity):string
    string json = obj.ser;                   Serializes any type inheriting from IUser to json string.
}
```

When working with generics, try to narrow down the types the method will apply to by using the `where` clause unless you are certain that the method should apply to every data type available to the compiler.

In this recipe, you have have learned generics behave with extension methods with a few things to watch out for and ways to work around them.

Extension methods with lambda expressions (Become an expert)

Lambda expressions are used in place of anonymous methods and delegates. They are used extensively in the LINQ namespace and other enumerated data types for their readability of condition matching.

Getting ready

Refer to the `ArrayExtensions.cs` and `FuncExtensions.cs` file in the `ExtensionMethods.Library` project for the extension methods. These methods are used in the `Program.cs` file in the `ExtensionMethods.Console` project.

How to do it...

The following code snippet shows an overloaded extension method `ToList()` which accepts a mapping function as a lambda expression:

```csharp
public static class ArrayExtensions
{
    /// <summary>
    /// Converts an array of items to List<T> using a mapping function
    /// </summary>
    /// <typeparam name="T"></typeparam>
    /// <param name="items"></param>
    /// <param name="mapFunction"></param>
    /// <remarks>Taken from http://www.extensionmethod.net/csharp/
array/tolist-t-func-object-t-func</remarks>
    /// <returns></returns>
    public static List<T> ToList<T>(this Array items, Func<object, T> mapFunction)
    {
        if (items == null || mapFunction == null)
            return new List<T>();

        List<T> coll = new List<T>();
        for (int i = 0; i < items.Length; i++)
        {
            T val = mapFunction(items.GetValue(i));
            if (val != null)
                coll.Add(val);
        }
        return coll;
    }
}
```

The following code is another extension method that focuses on extending a lambda expression or function to memorize the execution if the data is the same:

```
public static class FuncExtensions
{
    /// <summary>
    /// Memoize a function
    /// </summary>
    /// <typeparam name="T"></typeparam>
    /// <typeparam name="TResult"></typeparam>
    /// <param name="func">the function to memoize</param>
    /// <remarks>http://www.extensionmethod.net/csharp/func/memoize-t-
tresult</remarks>
    /// <returns></returns>
    public static Func<T, TResult> Memoize<T, TResult>(this Func<T,
TResult> func)
    {
        var t = new Dictionary<T, TResult>();
        return n =>
        {
            if (t.ContainsKey(n)) return t[n];
            else
            {
                var result = func(n);
                t.Add(n, result);
                return result;
            }
        };
    }
}
```

The following code shows the use of the extension methods:

```
private static void DoTaskEleven()
{
    Func<string, string> format = new Func<string, string>(s =>
    {
        // a long running operation
        System.Threading.Thread.Sleep(2000);
        return String.Format("hello {0}", s);
    }).Memoize();
    // takes 2000 ms
```

```
        for (int a = 0; a < 100;a++ )
        {
            System.Console.WriteLine(format(" world"));
        }
    }

    private static void DoTaskElevenPart2()
    {
        User[] users = new User[]
                        {
                            new User
                            {
                                FirstName = "Shawn",
                                LastName = "Mclean"
                            },
                            new User
                            {
                                FirstName = "Derron",
                                LastName = "Brown"
                            }
                        };
        var userVMs = users.ToList<UserViewModel>(o =>
                        {
                            var item = (User) o;
                            return new UserViewModel
                            {
                                FullName = (item).GetFullName(),
                                    UserId = item.UserId
                            };
                        });
    }
```

How it works...

The first code snippet, `ToList()`, is an extension of the array object which takes a mapping lambda expression function as a parameter. This function is then used to convert the values of the array to the type specified in the template definition. When calling this extension method, we simply apply the class type to the template and pass in the expression as a parameter as seen in the `DoTaskElevenPart2()` method in the use cases code snippet

```
    users.ToList<UserViewModel>(o => ...
```

The second code snippet, `Memoize()`, is an extension to the `Func` type. This is an extension method that does not incorporate lambda expressions as parameters but actually extends it. This use case is rare because there are usually better design patterns to use to accomplish the solution. In this method, we `Memoize` the value passed to the expression to prevent further processing, if it has already been called with that same data before.

The `DoTaskEleven()` snippet shows the body of the expression containing a `sleep` function that should take 2 seconds to execute. When `Memoize` is attached, if the method was already executed before with the same parameters, the body will never get executed again and the return value is returned from the cache, a dictionary in this case.

In this recipe, you have learned how to use lambda expressions to help make your extensions more flexible and also how to extend an actual lambda expression.

Structuring your project and best practices (Should know)

When using extension methods, it is good to set out a convention for your project in which your team will follow. This recipe seeks to demonstrate a few best practices and conventions that should get the project to a state where it can be easily maintained and worked on by other team members.

Getting ready

Refer to the Visual Studio solution `ExtensionMethods`.

How to do it...

Extensions normally go into a class library or a folder dedicated to just extension methods. The files and classes are named after the type they extend.

The following screenshot shows how a solution is usually structured after adding many more types of extensions:

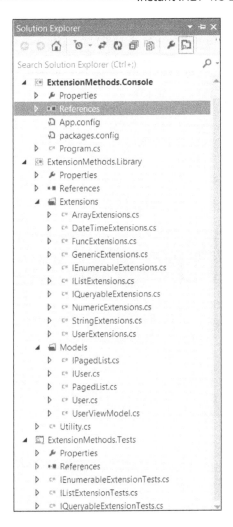

How it works...

There are a few practices and conventions that should guide you when using extension methods in your projects:

- ▶ **Own namespace**: Extension methods should be in their own namespace. By making your extensions pluggable, you allow the user to include or exclude them from the rest of the library. This allows the user to remove and add their own implementation as they wish. A good convention would be to place them in a namespace, such as `MyCompany.Common.Extensions`.

- ▶ **Be careful of extending types you do not own**: Changes to types you do not own may occur and cause changes that may break your extension methods.

▸ **Prioritize extension of interfaces over classes:** As a class developer, you can think of interfaces as immutable. If an interface changes, you can expect that all classes implementing from that interface will also be broken. However, this is still possible, the chances of an interface being modified are less likely.

▸ **Be specific:** Extensions on less specific types are more likely to be broken by external change than extensions on more specific types. This is because the higher a type is in the hierarchy, the more types there are that derive from it. An extension method on `Object` type can be broken by the introduction of any member to any type anywhere. An extension method on string, on the other hand, can only be broken by changes to string or other extension methods.

In this recipe, you have learned a few best practices, dos and don'ts of extension methods.

Appendix – List of well-known extension libraries

There are many libraries on the Internet which contain all varieties of extension methods, ranging from extending strings to IQueryable. This recipe seeks to give libraries and websites that contains a list of useful extension methods that you may use freely in your projects. The following are a list of extensions:

▸ **ExtensionMethod.net:** This website (`http://www.extensionmethod.net/`) contains a list of user submitted extension methods that contain both the source code of the extension and the use cases:

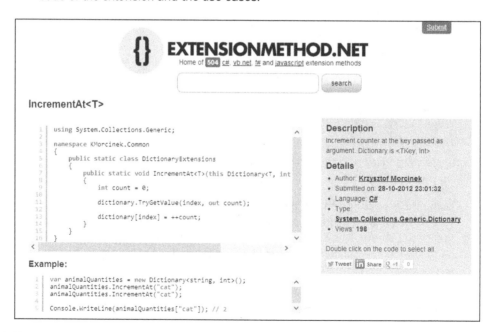

▸ **MoreLINQ**: MoreLINQ (`https://code.google.com/p/morelinq/`) is an open source library aimed at adding extra desirable features to LINQ to objects or simply put, LINQ in general. Some extensions include `TakeUntil`, `ExceptBy`, and `MatchBy`.

▸ **Reactive Extensions**: The Reactive Extensions (`http://msdn.microsoft.com/en-us/data/gg577609.aspx`) is a library for composing asynchronous and event-based programs using observable sequences and LINQ-style query operators.

▸ **dotNetExt**: dotNetExt (`http://dotnetext.codeplex.com/`) is an open source library with extension methods ranging from `Boolean`, `DateTime`, `TimeSpan` to collections such as `IEnumerable`. Some extensions include `EndOfMonth()` on `DateTime.Now` and Encrypt<Algorithm>/Decrypt<Algorithm> for bytes.

The following image shows the library availability on NuGet package manager:

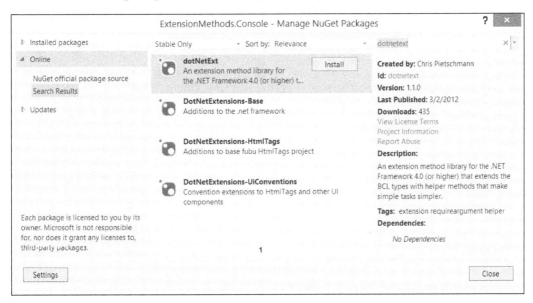

▸ **.NET extension methods library for C# and VB.NET**: This open source library is, currently, the most comprehensive extension methods library. It contains hundreds of extensions, ranging from the extension of core .NET classes, ASP.NET, ASP.NET MVC, WPF, and WinForms classes.

Site URL: `http://dnpextensions.codeplex.com/`. By using what we learned from earlier recipes, it is up to the developer to reference these libraries in their project and simply calls these extensions. Some of these libraries will be available on NuGet package explorer and can easily be pulled down into your projects through package manager.

Thus, you have access to a few existing extension methods that should immediately become useful in your projects.

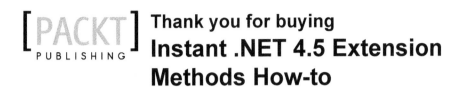

Thank you for buying
Instant .NET 4.5 Extension Methods How-to

About Packt Publishing

Packt, pronounced 'packed', published its first book "*Mastering phpMyAdmin for Effective MySQL Management*" in April 2004 and subsequently continued to specialize in publishing highly focused books on specific technologies and solutions.

Our books and publications share the experiences of your fellow IT professionals in adapting and customizing today's systems, applications, and frameworks. Our solution based books give you the knowledge and power to customize the software and technologies you're using to get the job done. Packt books are more specific and less general than the IT books you have seen in the past. Our unique business model allows us to bring you more focused information, giving you more of what you need to know, and less of what you don't.

Packt is a modern, yet unique publishing company, which focuses on producing quality, cutting-edge books for communities of developers, administrators, and newbies alike. For more information, please visit our website: www.packtpub.com.

Writing for Packt

We welcome all inquiries from people who are interested in authoring. Book proposals should be sent to author@packtpub.com. If your book idea is still at an early stage and you would like to discuss it first before writing a formal book proposal, contact us; one of our commissioning editors will get in touch with you.

We're not just looking for published authors; if you have strong technical skills but no writing experience, our experienced editors can help you develop a writing career, or simply get some additional reward for your expertise.

ASP.NET 4 Social Networking

ISBN: 978-1-84969-082-9   Paperback: 484 pages

A truly hands-on book for ASP.NET 4 Developers

1. Create a full-featured, enterprise-grade social network using ASP.NET 4.0

2. Learn key new ASP.NET and .NET Framework concepts like Managed Extensibility Framework (MEF), Entity Framework 4.0, LINQ, AJAX, C# 4.0, ASP.NET Routing,n-tier architectures, and MVP in a practical, hands-on way

3. Build friends lists, messaging systems, user profiles, blogs, forums, groups, and more

4. A practical guide full of step by step explanations, interesting examples, and practical advice

NHibernate 3 Beginner's Guide

ISBN: 978-1-84951-602-0   Paperback: 368 pages

Rapidly retrieve data from your database into .NET objects

1. Incorporate robust, efficient data access into your .Net projects

2. Reduce hours of application development time and get better application architecture and performance

3. Create your domain model first and then derive the database structure automatically from the model

4. Test, profile, and monitor data access to tune the performance and make your applications fly

Please check **www.PacktPub.com** for information on our titles

Entity Framework Tutorial

ISBN: 978-1-84719-522-7   Paperback: 228 pages

Learn to build a better data access layer with the ADO. NET entity Framework and ADO.NET Data Services

1. Clear and concise guide to the ADO.NET Entity Framework with plentiful code examples

2. Create Entity Data Models from your database and use them in your applications

3. Learn about the Entity Client data provider and create statements in Entity SQL

4. Learn about ADO.NET Data Services and how they work with the Entity Framework

Entity Framework 4.1: Expert's Cookbook

ISBN: 978-1-84968-446-0   Paperback: 352 pages

More than 40 recipes for successfully mixing Test Driven Development, Architecture, and Entity Framework Code First

1. Hands-on solutions with reusable code examples

2. Strategies for enterprise ready usage

3. Examples based on real world experience

4. Detailed and advanced examples of query management

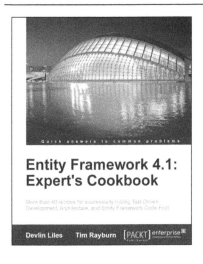

Please check **www.PacktPub.com** for information on our titles